What can you see in this l
Can you see some blobs o

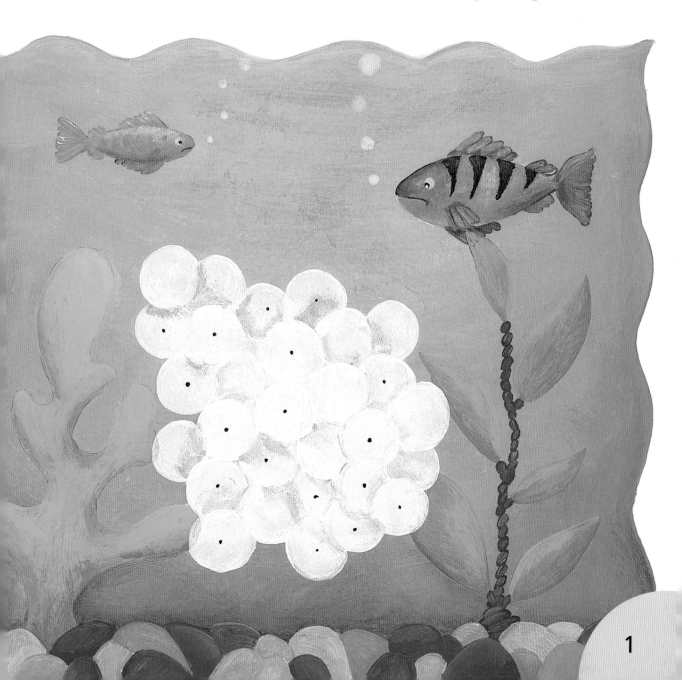

Can you see some black dots inside the jelly? Those dots are tiny eggs.

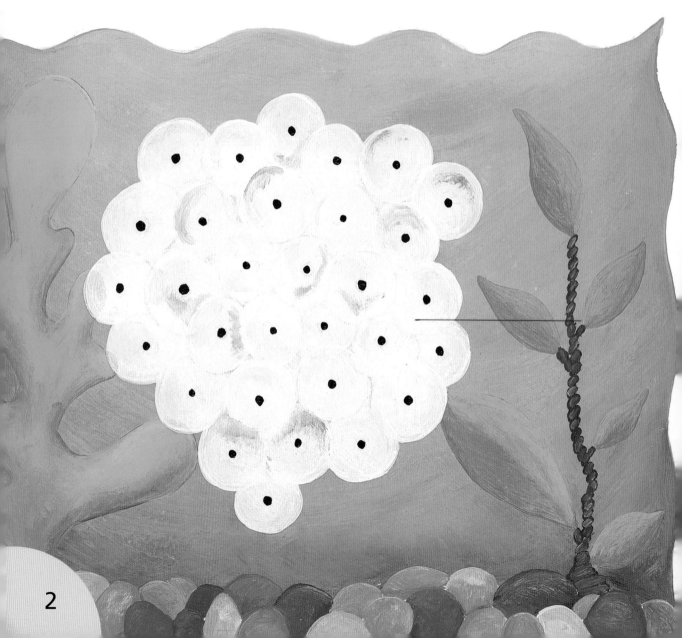

The dots grow. The jelly shrinks.

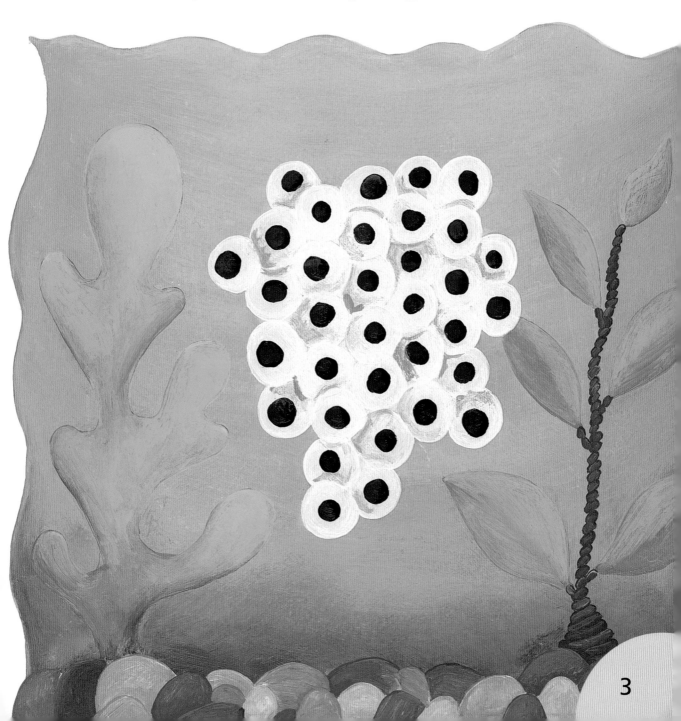

The dots are growing tails. They are baby tadpoles!

The tadpoles are tiny. They stick to the weeds.

Then they begin to swim.

Quick, tadpoles, swim away!
Here comes a big fish!

The fish eats some of the tadpoles.

The rest swim away. They hide in the weeds.

Can you see some bumps on this tadpole? Those bumps will be legs.

These tadpoles only have
back legs.

This tadpole has all its legs.
Its tail is shrinking.

This tadpole has no tail.

The tadpole kicks with its legs.
It jumps out of the lake.

But is it a tadpole?

No, it's a frog!